AuthorHouse™
1663 Liberty Drive
Bloomington, IN 47403
www.authorhouse.com
Phone: 833-262-8899

This book is printed on acid-free paper.

ISBN: 978-1-6655-6999-6 (sc)
ISBN: 978-1-6655-7000-8 (e)

Library of Congress Control Number: 2022916458

Print information available on the last page.

Published by AuthorHouse 10/06/2022

authorHOUSE®

Contents

PREFACE

Parents for a Global Influence of the Church

How has the growth of Christianity trended in the past few decades? In his recent article, 'Decline of Christianity Shows No Signs of Stopping,' Daniel Silliman (2022) in Christianity Today made the following observation from a PEW research study that projects that the religious identity of Christianity in the US will drop below 50 percent by 2070:

> The data they do have, from 50 years of research by the General Social Survey and Pew's own survey of 15,000 adults in 2019, indicates the current trend is inexorable. People are giving up on Christianity. They will continue to do so. And if you're trying to predict the future religious landscape in America, according to Pew, the question is not whether Christianity will decline. It's how fast and how far.

In a further observation, Silliman (2022) makes the following comments:

> Currently, 64 percent of people say they are Christian, but nearly a third of those raised Christian eventually switch to "none" or "nothing in particular," while only about 20 percent of those raised without religion become Christian. If that ratio of switching continues at a steady pace, then in roughly half a century, only about 46 percent of Americans will identify as Christian. If the rate of switching continues to accelerate, as it has since the 1990s, the percent calling themselves Christians will drop to 35.

In the light of what seems to be an inexorable trend of decline in the identity of Christianity in America, how Christian parents can help advance the Church's global influence, by her witness of Christ is the pursuit of this work. It is all in the diligent collective leadership parents will give to the development of the early childhood Christian formation of the children that God gives them, starting from the womb (at conception), the formative years, into their young adulthood.

Parents are the first recipients of every child who joins our societies, communities, and institutions. What they do to and with the child's early childhood Christian formation development is vital to the advancement of the Church's witness of Christ in homes, churches, schools, work, and marketplaces, before any other significant person or institution receives them. In addition is what that gives to the strengthening of a people's moral and ethics capital, for the overall good of their society, community, or neighborhood.

I am touching on the idea of Christian parents' leadership in what they do to and with their God given children in the development of their early childhood Christian formation. I see in this spectrum of Christian parents' leadership a path to the Church's effectual Global influence – in a world culture, needing the witness of Christ more than ever before. *How is this so?* First, let me bring out John C. Maxwell's[1] central idea of what leadership is. I will build on Maxwell's principal idea of leadership to assemble the type of leadership that Christian parents are to give to the development of the early childhood Christian formation of their own children. It will identify the need for this book, *'The 6 Habits of Highly Effective Parents.'*

For Maxwell, leadership is simply influence (2011, p.2). He proposes that *"If people can increase their influence with others, they can lead more effectively,"* (Maxwell, 2011, p.2). How people can increase their influence with others, so they can lead effectively has been a part of Maxwell's distinguished work on leadership. I am more interested in Maxwell's notion of leadership as influence. Influence itself is to be understood as *"the capacity to have an effect on the character, development, or behavior of someone,"* (google.com).

How is Maxwell's indication of leadership as *'influence'* applicable in Christian parents' leadership, concerning the early childhood Christian formation of their own children? This preface shows in brief how that *'influence'* is to playout in Christian parent's Leadership, concerning the early childhood Christian formation of their own children, starting from the womb (at conception), the formative years, into their young adulthood.

Christian parents' leadership as an influence in the early childhood Christian formation of their own children is to be guided by the idealism of Christian formation. In Dr. Mills' words, *"the idealism of Christian formation is the art and science in forming the mindset and the emotional asset (the attitude set) of a child to become a member of the body of Christ, hence, the bride of*

---

[1] Maxwell, J. C. (2011). The 5 Levels of Leadership: Proven Steps to Maximize Potential: Center Street.

Christ; so that in adulthood, the individual has a formed lifestyle of strong consciousness for the personal presence and influence of God in the management of their Christian lives."

Based on Dr. Mills' idealism of Christian formation, Christian parents' leadership development is therefore the resources, tools, frameworks, and the inspiration that Church Principals and or institutions, (*such as Pastors, Focus of the Family, the Global Institute for Christian Living and Growth*) would make available for Christian parents, to build their skill sets, for affecting the early childhood Christian formation of their own children, to become one with Christ, as a member of his body, hence the bride; with the goal that the children will grow in having a strong influence of God in their day-to-day Christian living. So that in a recap, the goal for early childhood Christian formation is the development of the child's consciousness to have the influence of God in their Christian living.

THE GOAL FOR EARLY CHILDHOOD CHRISTIAN FORMATION

GOAL

▪ The developed consciousness for the influence of God in the child's life

Dr. Mills

Figure 1. The developmental goal of early childhood Christian formation.

The above indications are to the point that a developed lifestyle of strong consciousness and conscientiousness of the personal presence and influence of God corresponds to the person's witness of Christ in their immediate settings. The witness of Christ itself is to be noted as a behavior that portrays the lifestyle of Christ that radiates the influence of God, the Father in his life. Christ says of himself, *"When ye have lifted up the Son of man, then shall ye know that I am he, and that I do nothing of myself; but as my Father hath taught me, I speak these things. And he that sent me is with me: The Father hath not left me alone; for I do always those things that please him,"* (John 8:28-29). Perhaps, it is this truth about Christ that reveals him as the Light that shines in the darkness and that the darkness is not able to comprehend it (John 1:4-9). Of his persona as the LIGHT, which is from the personal influence of God, the Father, Christ's way of living in his person as man will always end in decisions and choices that are morally and ethically good to the glory of the Father. This is the emblem of Christ's life that counters or will counter the DARKNESS of social vices, in all their forms and manifestations.

With these indications concerning the personal influence of God and the witness of the Christ life, I am heading to the point that a collective force of Christian parents' influence in the early childhood Christian formation of their own children will produce a collective force of people with strong personal influence of God in the management of their Christian lives. A collective force of people with strong personal influence of God in the management of their Christian lives is an exhibition of the witness of the Christ life that will have a dominating influence over anti-Christian values that are in great ascendancy in the world today.

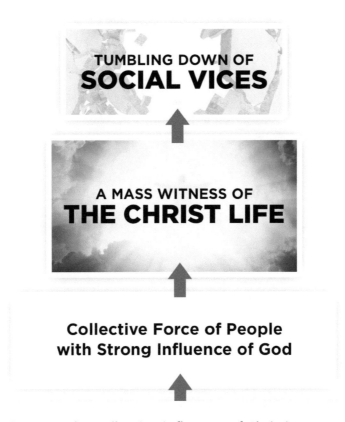

Figure 2. The collective influence of Christian parents'
leadership and the countering of social vices.

Christian parents, therefore, can advance the Church's global influence by her witness of Christ, when they have a collective capacity of influence in the early childhood Christian formation of their own children into their young adulthood.

Over here, Maxwell's proposition that *"If people can increase their influence with others, they can lead more effectively"* (2011, p.2), would lend credence to Dr. Mills' Parents' Competencies Matrix in the idea that a positive correlation exists between parents' competency in Christian formation and the effectiveness of their parenting and how that would impact the children's success in managing their Christian life.

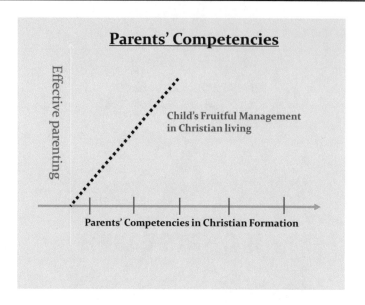

Graph 1. Dr. Mills' Parents' Competencies Matrix.

As the Diagram suggests, Parents' competence in Christian formation would yield in highly effective parenting that is efficient to help the children succeed in the management of their Christian life.

It is Maxwell's leadership as influence proposition and Dr. Mills' Parents' Competencies Matrix that give prudence for the quest to boost the capacity of Christian parents' leadership in the early childhood Christian formation of their own children, starting from the womb (at conception), the formative years, into their young adulthood. It is the path to seeing the global impact of the Church, by her witness of the lifestyle of Christ.

A pursuit of boosting the collective capacity of Christian parents' leadership in the early childhood Christian formation of their own children, for a global influence of the Church is the creation of this book – 'The 6 Habits of Highly Effective Parents.' It is prepared to give parents a six-point-principles to gain the mental attitudes and the inclinations that would help them carry their God-given mandate as the Primary Ministers of God, for the evangelizing and the discipling of their own children. A ministry that starts from the womb, through the formative years of the children, into their young adulthood.

INTRODUCTION

The Purpose of the Book

- The purpose of this book is to guide you as parents, to process and to internalize each of the 6-Point Principles of Christian Parenting, as habits of a highly effective parent
- It is to help you come to full grips with the practical importance of Christian parenting in God's scheme to honor Christ with preeminence/supremacy, as the head of his body
- It will grant you a clear picture that will help you visualize your critical role as parents, who are to serve as the primary ministers of God, in the scheme of God's work for bringing your child into the world
- You will learn this to be a critical role God had set up in creation as part of his eternal purpose in Christ, concerning his oneness with the Church, to be his body and his bride
- You will know God set it up for you to influence the early childhood Christian formation of your own child, starting from the womb, through the formative years, into their young adulthood
- You will know that your critical influence in the early childhood Christian formation of your child is for them to know and to live in their identity as the bride of Christ, and to have a strong influence of God in their Christian living, as a lifestyle

The Goals of the Book

The goals of the book are for you to:

1. Know and to reckon that you are the primary ministers of God for the development of the early childhood Christian formation of your own child, starting from the womb, through the formative years, into their young adulthood

2. Gain the understanding that you are God's steward of the child he is bringing into the world by you as parents, to fulfill his mission and objectives concerning the forming of Christ's oneness with the Church, to be his body and bride

3. Have the mental attitude and an inclined persuasion to parent your child into the identity (the body and the bride of Christ) and the lifestyle (the life Christ modeled while on earth) that God had set, for bringing them into the world, by you

4. Come to terms with the demand that your effectual parenting requires routine things to do to and with the child to develop the appropriate habits due for their successful or a thriving Christian living in adulthood; that sets them up for rewards in eternity

5. See and value the importance in your commitment to engage in parenting the child together as a teamwork with your spouse, where it applies

6. Have the openness to parenting skills development, which is a Christian leadership attitude in response to 2 Timothy 2:15; *"Study to shew thyself approved unto God, a workman that needs not to be ashamed..."*

7. Boost your parenting responsiveness to the early childhood Christian formation of your own child

The Objectives of the Book

At the end of this book, you will be able to:

- Know and speak to the critical role of parents in God's scheme of work for the advancement of the Church's witness of Christ in homes, churches, schools, work, and marketplaces
- Know, explain, and give value to each of the 6-Point Principles of Christian Parenting, as habits of a highly effective parent
- Know and be able to assess the collective value of the 6-Point Principles of Christian Parenting in relation to the importance of Christian formation

Personal Growth Assessment

At the end of each chapter, a personal growth assessment is provided for you to journal the lessons that you have gained from the sections of the study.

Critical Question

What are we to learn from each of the 6-Point Principles of Christian Parenting?

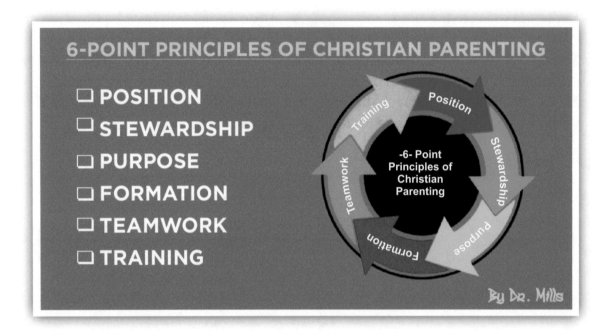

Figure 3. A mapping for lessons in the six-point principles of Christian parenting.

We will now discuss in the next six lessons each of the 6-point principles of Christian parenting, as habits of a highly effective parent.

CHAPTER 1

POSITION

You are God's Portal for the Child's Entrance into the World

<u>Please take a moment to observe the following portrait</u> - A scheme of God's work in his formation of Christ's oneness with the Church, to be his body and bride.

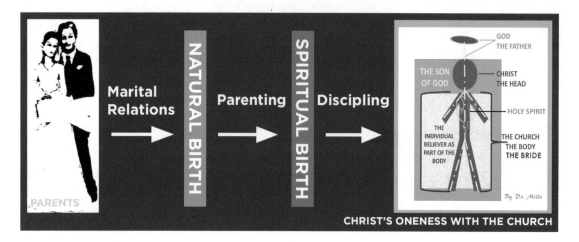

Figure 4. The position of parents in God's scheme of work for
the formation of Christ's oneness with the Church.

- The portrait is to help you visualize your position as parents, who serve as God's portals in the scheme of his work in forming Christ's oneness with the Church, to be his body and bride
- The scheme is based on Romans 8:28-29
- We will do an analytical breakdown of Romans 8:28:29, to give you the biblical perspective on why God created your parenting position as the portal, in bringing your child into the world

An Analytical Breakdown of Romans 8:28-29

And we know that all things work together for good to them that love God, to them who are the called according to his purpose. For whom he did foreknow, he also did predestinate to be conformed to the image of his Son, that he might be the firstborn among many brethren.

- In verse 28, Paul points out those who are *'the called'* implying the Church. The Church is *'the called'* according to God's purpose
- Also note that the Church is the set of humanity whom God will spiritually give birth to, by the incorruptible seed of Christ (1 Peter 1:23), to be formed in oneness with the person of Christ as man, who are to be his body and bride

As one who is to become a member of the body and the bride of Christ, your child is designated or ordained to be a member of the Church. For this study, we can say your child is the 'church,' by reason that a slice of cake is still cake - the properties of the parts are the same as the whole.

- Verse 28 that mentions 'the called' (the Church) according to *God's purpose* provides the context for verse 29
- The nature of the purpose of God mentioned in verse 28 is then explained in verse 29. And to get to the understanding of the nature of that purpose, we will discuss verse 29 in a three-part Illustration

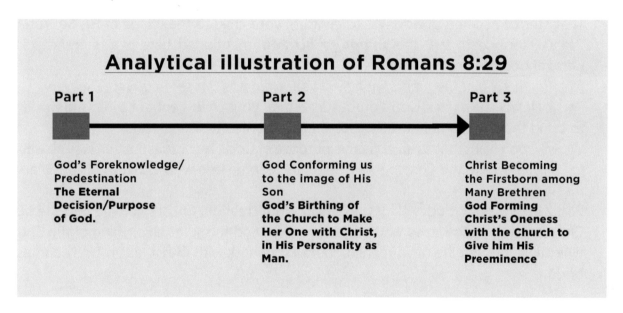

Figure 5. A three-part analytical breakdown of Romans 8:29.

Part 1

- The Bible says in Ephesians 1:4, *according as he has chosen us in him before the foundation of the world*
- Part 1 is God's foreknowledge and the predestination of the Church (your child). And this speaks to the eternal decision/purpose that God made concerning the life of your child/ the Church, before the world began

<u>A Guiding Question</u>

What was the nature of this eternal decision or purpose of God?

- It has a two-fold or an inclusive purpose, hence part 2 and part 3

Part 2

- Part 2 gives the nature of the eternal decision/purpose that God made concerning the life of your child/the Church, before the beginning of the world
- That eternal decision of God was to conform your child to the image of His Son/Christ
- We will soon learn that the '***image of his Son***' mentioned here is a reference to the personhood of Christ as man
- *Note in Part 2 that the predestination of your child was not set to a place (heaven)*
- Part 2 clearly shows that God's predestination of your child's entrance into the world was to bring them into a union with Jesus Christ - a person not a place!!!
- We will soon learn that as an objective purpose of God, the predestination was essentially, to spiritually birth the Church (your child), to become one with Christ as his body and as his bride
- Part 2 involves or includes all of God's work from creation, Christ's coming into the world, Christ's death on the cross, and his resurrection, and the spiritual birthing of the Church, which includes the life of your child, to have oneness with Christ, as his body and as his bride

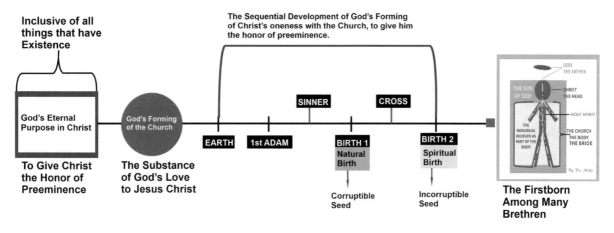

Figure 6. The sequential development of God's work from creation to the formation of Christ's oneness with the Church, to be his body and bride.

- Simply put, the key target in the eternal purpose that God purposed for bringing your child into the world was to make them have oneness with Christ, in his spiritual personality as man

We will now discuss what the image of his Son means.

A Critical Question

What does the image of His Son mean?

- The answer to this question is to help you understand that the *image of his Son* in Romans 8:29 refers to the spiritual personality of Christ as man
- It will help you to see that God's mission for your child's oneness with Christ is purposed to be in the spiritual personality of Christ as man, which in God's wisdom will also make it necessary for Christ to come into the world as man
- It will also help you to see that a central objective of your parenting is the influence you give to your child, from the womb, through their formative years, to come into the humanity of Christ, which occurs when they are spiritually birthed by God

Figure 7. The four key milestones of human development in Christian formation.

- It is also to help you see that God's spiritual birth of your child to have oneness with Christ is an essential milestone of your child's human development. Without the spiritual birth, your child's human development is not complete

Achieving the Meaning of the 'Image of His Son'

- The New Testament scriptures reveal Jesus Christ as **fully God** (John 1:1, Hebrews 1:8-10, Philippians 2:6), and **fully man** (John 1:14, Philippians 2:5-8, 1 Timothy 3:16, Hebrews 2:11-17)

John 1:1-2

In the beginning was the Word, and the Word was with God, and the Word was God. The same was in the beginning with God.

Philippians 2:5-8

Let this mind be in you, which was also in Christ Jesus: Who, being in the form of God, thought it not robbery to be equal with God: But made himself of no reputation, and took upon him the form of a servant, and was made in the likeness of men: And being found in fashion as a man, he humbled himself, and became obedient unto death, even the death of the cross.

- The above scriptural indications are the reference points to the personhood of Christ as fully God and fully man

Figure 8. The two personalities of Christ – both fully God and fully man.

- Since Jesus Christ is fully man, the *'image of His Son'* in relation to the Church being human will speak to the personality of Christ as man and not to his deity (as God)
- The claim that the *'image of his Son'* is the personality of Christ as man is verified by the text's description of the Church as the *'brethren'* of Christ
- Since the brethren are human, Christ as the firstborn among many brethren must also be human to make the nature of the association credible (**Hebrews 2:12-14**)

Hebrews 2:12-14

For both he that sanctifies, and they who are sanctified are all of one: for which cause he is not ashamed to call them brethren, saying, I will declare thy name unto my brethren, in the midst of the church will I sing praise unto thee. And again, I will put my trust in him. And again, Behold I and the children which God hath given me. Forasmuch then as the children are partakers of flesh and blood, he also himself likewise took part of the same.

A Critical Question

How are we conformed to the image of his Son/Christ by God?

- As Jesus Christ was born by God by the power of the Holy Spirit to take on his personality as man (the last and true Adam), so is the Church born anew by God by the power of the Holy Spirit to become one with Christ in his spiritual personality as man
- The Bible indicates, *as we have borne the image of the first Adam, we shall also bear the image of the Last Adam, who is Jesus Christ, the Lord* (1 Corinthians 15:45-49)
- Typically, the Church gets to bear the personality of Christ as man, by her spiritual birthing by God to also become His 'son'

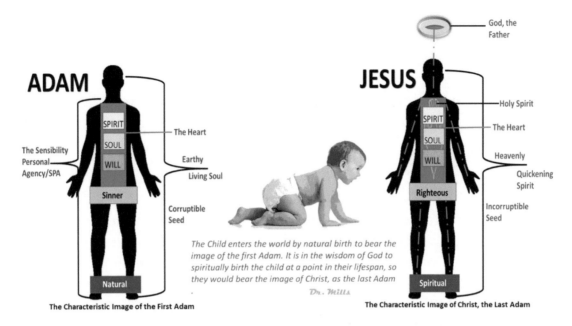

Figure 9. The distinctive personality make-up of the first Adam, and Christ as the last Adam.

- The Bible also indicates, *"but as many as received him, to them gave he power to become the sons of God, even to them that believe on his name: which were born, not of blood, nor of the will of the flesh, nor of the will of man, but of God,"* (John 1:12-13)

Figure 7. The four key milestones of human development in Christian formation.

- It seems imperative that from conception through the natural birth, the child is to be spiritually birthed by God as a milestone in their human development, which makes them one with Christ, in his spiritual personality as man
- In effect, this is what conformed to the *image of his Son* means – God's spiritual birthing of the Church to become His 'son,' for them to have their union with Christ in his spiritual personality as man; and it is only an essential part of the eternal purpose of God, for why he is bringing your child into the world, which brings us to the third part of Romans 8:29

Part 3

- Part 3 gives the nature of the eternal decision/purpose that God made concerning **Christ**, which speaks to his preeminence/supremacy as the firstborn among many brethren
- Christ receives his preeminence/supremacy as the firstborn among many brethren, only when the Church is conformed to his image, which is his personality as man
- It is important to see the link between Part 2 and Part 3. *"for whom he did foreknow, he also did predestinate to be conformed to the image of his Son, that **he** might be the firstborn among many brethren"*
- The pronoun '**he**' which refers to Christ, the 'Son' is the link between the two Parts
- It means that the eternal purpose of God concerning the Church getting conformed to the image of his Son is not a terminal event/outcome. It is not an end of itself
- It is tied or linked to the ultimate eternal purpose of God in Christ, which is the preeminence/supremacy of Christ as the firstborn among many brethren.
- **Without Part 2, Part 3 will not happen**

Critical Question

In what terms are you to view the preeminence/supremacy of Christ, as the firstborn among many brethren?

- Since the preeminence/supremacy of Christ as the firstborn among many brethren is the ultimate eternal purpose of God, it also serves as the driving point of God that makes the events of Part 1 and Part 2 necessary and compelling things to take place
- The preeminence/supremacy of Christ as the firstborn among many brethren must be looked at as the eternal vision or the main purpose of God. That is what warranted all things to take place
- God's work regarding creation, Christ's coming into the world, Christ's death on the cross and his resurrection; and the spiritual birthing of the Church to have oneness with Christ as his body and as his bride are all the objective things purposed to happen in that order. So, that Christ will receive his preeminence/supremacy as the firstborn among many brethren
- The conforming to the image of His Son must then be looked at as **God's mission** for bringing the Church (your child) into the world to have oneness with Christ
- The spiritual birthing is to be looked at as **God's objective** thing to do concerning your child, to fulfill his mission for them to have the oneness with Christ, which would then give Christ his preeminence/supremacy, as the firstborn among many brethren

Why God is Bringing your Child into the World

Mission
God's mission for bringing your child into the world is to have him/her come into oneness with Christ, in His personality as man.

Objective
God's objective for bringing your child into the world is to spiritually give birth to him/her, to have oneness with Christ in His Sonship.

Vision
God's vision for bringing your child into the world is ultimately to honor Christ with status of preeminence, as the firstborn among many brethren.

Figure 10. God's statement of purpose for bringing your child into the world.

- In effect, the ultimate eternal purpose of God for bringing your child into the world is first based on the eternal decision to honor Christ with the status of preeminence/supremacy, as the firstborn among many brethren, before the world began. That decision included the mission (for the child to have oneness with Christ) and the main objective (to spiritually give birth to your child to become his son). These are the two main benchmarks upon which Christ will receive His preeminence as the firstborn among many brethren

A Critical Question

How is God bringing the child into the world to form them in oneness with Christ?

(**I will like you to ponder on this question for a moment**)

- Obviously, God is not going to throw them from heaven or from somewhere in the universe into the world

(**Let us do a recall of the portrait scheme**)

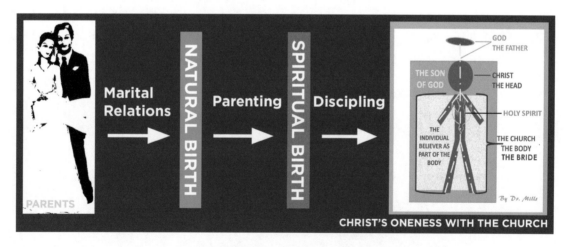

Figure 4. The position of parents in God's scheme of work for the formation of Christ's oneness with the Church.

The Essential/Critical Role of Parents as God's Portals for His Eternal Purpose in Christ

- Do you realize your position as parents? Do you see it as the portal, the gateway by which God is bringing 'your' child into the world, to be formed in oneness with Christ, as a member of the Church?
- As parents, your position as a portal for the entrance of 'your' child into the world is not a random occurrence
- It is a natural positioning that God specifically put in place in creation. It has a similar value for human existence, as does the air we breathe
- That human existence cannot survive on earth, without air, it is also true that without the positioning of parents in creation, human existence cannot take place on earth, since parents are God's portals for the entrance of mankind into the world
- As God has ordered things to be in creation for certain specific functions, he has also rendered it certain in creation that without parents, his objective for forming Christ's oneness with the Church cannot happen. In other words, Romans 8:29 will be a thing out of the window, without you as parents
- Without you as parents, 'your' child cannot come into the world. They cannot have human existence, and God cannot have them, for the formation of Christ's oneness with the Church
- As parents, your position as God's portal for the entrance of 'your' child into the world is a God valued position of influence in the life of your child, for him to realize his mission, the objective, and the eternal vision for bringing them into the world
- I trust that as you ponder over your valued position of influence in the life of your child, you will come to grips with your critical role in God's overall scheme of work for the formation of Christ's oneness with the Church
- I trust that it will increase your eagerness in giving the due diligence to your critical role in the early childhood Christian formation of your own children

A thing to Consider

That human existence cannot survive on earth, without air, it is also true that without the positioning of parents in creation, human existence cannot take place on earth, since parents are God's portals for the entrance of mankind into the world.

True or False

Discussion

Please discuss with your spouse, lessons from your position as parents in the life of your child if it applies.

PERSONAL GROWTH ASSESSMENT

Please write in the space provided the lessons that you have gained from this chapter of your study

_____

_____

_____

_____

_____

_____

_____

_____

_____

_____

_____

CHAPTER 2

STEWARDSHIP

The Child Belongs to God, Not You

- As God's portal for the entrance of 'your' child into the world, the logic follows that the ownership of the child is God's and not yours
- The Bible says: "*Lo, children are a heritage of the Lord,*" (Psalm 127:3)
- Google.com defines heritage as *property that is or may be inherited.* As suggested by the scripture, the definition of heritage points to children as God's property

- As one would put it, children are God's property and that he uses parents as *the means* to inherit them
- It is also of God to use parents to take care of his property, as stewards of influence, for the children to come into what he has ordained their lives to be on earth

Please do a Reading of John 17:6

*I have manifested thy name unto the men which thou gave me out of the world: **thine they were, and thou gave them me;** and they have kept thy word.*

Critical Comments

- Do you realize what Jesus is saying about his disciples? They belonged to God, and he gave them to him
- I wonder how much their parents knew that about them, that they belonged to God, and that they were God's stewards of their lives

<u>A Guiding Question</u>

What lessons can be gleaned from Sampson's parents that project the significance of this principle in Christian parenting?

Please do a Reading of Judges 13:2-12

Then Manoah intreated the LORD, and said, O my Lord, let the man of God which thou didst send come again unto us, and teach us what we shall do unto the child that shall be born.

The Lessons from Sampson's Parents

- Google.com defines stewardship as the job of supervising or taking care of something, such as an organization or property
- Merriam-webester.com defines stewardship as the conducting, supervising, or managing of something especially the careful and responsible management of something entrusted to one's care
- Manoah's intreating of God to know how-to parent the child into what he is to become, seems to pull out the acknowledgement of their stewardship of the child
- Perhaps as stewards of the child God was bringing to them, they had it in their parenting prospects, the mental attitude to develop in Sampson, the identity, and the lifestyle that God had purposed for him, not compromising that for their own personal preferences/ pleasures, or what their society would have him to become

The Lessons for Christian Parents

- By the example of Sampson's parents, a major principle in Christian parenting is in how the ownership of the child is viewed and valued. Christ's assessment of this value, the mental attitude of Sampson's parents are clear indications that a starting place for effectual parenting is the acknowledgement that the children God is bringing into the world by you as parents are his. They belong to God, and not you
- Your relationship and commitment to the child is to be defined as stewardship, a receiver and keeper of God's property
- **<u>Here is the key lesson</u>**: The degree of understanding of how much it sits in you that you are God's stewards of the child he is bringing into the world by you will correlate with the height of attention that you give to the parenting goals and objectives that God had set for their lives
- This brings up the next point of principle or habit that we are to give to parenting, which is the parenting of the child in the identity and the lifestyle that God had eternally purposed in bringing them into the world

A thing to Consider

Ben said to his son Joey; "I am your father. I brought you into this world. You are my son, and you will do what I am asking you to do. Do you hear me?"

In principle, Ben's projection of himself affirms the understanding that parents are God's stewards of the children he brings into the world.

True or False

Discussion

Please discuss with your spouse, Ben's sayings to his son, in the principle of your stewardship as parents to your children, if it applies.

PERSONAL GROWTH ASSESSMENT

Please write in the space provided the lessons that you have gained from this chapter of your study

_____

_____

_____

_____

_____

_____

_____

_____

_____

_____

_____

_____

CHAPTER 3

PURPOSE

The Child's Identity and Lifestyle is Already Set by God

Please do a Reading of the Following Recap

Note that parents are God's portal for the children's entrance into the world. The logic then follows that parents are God's stewards of the children he is bringing into the world. These two notions sum up in the principle that the parenting goals and objectives for the children are to be pinned on what God had purposed their lives to be in their oneness with Christ, before the foundation of the world.

A Guiding Question

What lessons can be gleaned from Sampson's parents that project the significance of this principle in Christian parenting?

The Example with Sampson's Parents

Please do a Reading of Judges 13:2-12

And there was a certain man of Zorah, of the family of the Danites, whose name was Manoah; and his wife was barren, and bare not. And the angel of the LORD appeared unto the woman, and said unto her, behold now, thou art barren, and bearest not: but thou shalt conceive, and bear a son. Now therefore beware, I pray thee, and drink not wine nor strong drink, and eat not any unclean thing: For, lo, thou shalt conceive, and bear a son; and no razor shall come on his head: **for the child shall be a Nazarite unto God from the womb: and he shall begin to deliver Israel out of the hand of the Philistines.***Then the woman came and told her husband, saying, A man of God came unto me, and his countenance was like the countenance of an angel of God, very terrible: but I asked him not whence he was, neither told he me his name: But he said unto me, behold, thou shalt conceive, and bear a son; and now drink no wine nor strong drink, neither eat any unclean thing: for the child shall be a Nazarite to God from the womb to the day of his death.* <u>*Then Manoah intreated the LORD, and said, O my Lord, let the man of God which thou didst send come again unto us, and teach us what we shall do unto the child that shall be born.*</u> *And God hearkened to the voice of Manoah; and the angel of God came again unto the woman as she sat in the field: but Manoah her husband was not with her. And the woman made haste, and ran, and shewed her husband, and said unto him, Behold, the man hath appeared unto me, that came unto me the other day. And Manoah arose, and went after his wife, and came to the man, and said unto him, Art thou the man that spoke unto the woman? And he said, I am. And Manoah said, Now let thy words come to pass. How shall we order the child, and how shall we do unto him?*

The Lessons from Sampson's Parents

- You do realize in the scripture, the keen attitude of Sampson's parents to know from God how and what they were to do to the promised child
- Besides the expectation to raise Sampson to observe the Law (God's regulations for the children of Israel in how they were to live their lives), their mental attitude shows a mission to know from God, the specific identity and lifestyle that they were to parent Sampson to become, to have, and to live
- It shows in their mental attitude that they were not largely interested in parenting Sampson to become what they personally wanted him to be, for their own pleasure and what lifestyle they personally wanted him to live, for their own honor
- Their mental attitude seemed to be parents who have the principle in their hearts to parent Sampson to come into the identity that God had ordained for him to be, and the lifestyle that God had desired for him to live
- As the Lord had commanded, the parents gave their due diligence to the parenting of Sampson, starting from the womb, through his early childhood formation into his young adulthood, to be and to live the lifestyle of a Nazarite to God
- That Sampson lived over twenty plus years of his life as a Nazarite unto God should give his parents full credits for their parenting influence in his early childhood formation – from the womb into his adulthood to be and to live the lifestyle as a Nazarite

The Lessons for Christian Parents

- By the example of Sampson's parents, a major principle in Christian parenting is to parent the child to come into the identity that God had ordained them to be, and to live the lifestyle that God had set for them, in their oneness with Christ

A Guiding Question

What identity and lifestyle had God already set for 'your' child, to be the principal guide in your Christian parenting?

- For Sampson's parents, they were to parent Sampson to be and to live as a Nazarite, which they did
- As Christian parents, the principle is to parent the child to know and to live as the bride of Christ
- We will soon learn that the bride of Christ is the description of the identity that God had designated for the child to be, in their oneness with Christ
- As Christian parents, it is also in the principle to parent the child to carry a strong consciousness for God's influence in their day-to-day Christian living. This is the lifestyle of Christ that he modeled for Christian living

A Scriptural Exploration that Shows God's Intent of your Child to be the Bride of Christ

Before we move to the next principle, I believe it is important to have an in-depth exploration, to gain the knowledge and the understanding that 'the Bride of Christ' is a description of the identity that God had designated your child to be, in the personality of Christ as man.

The goals for this in-depth exploration are to:

1. Help you to view and handle your child as the 'Bride of Christ'

2. Get you poised in developing the cognitive (mental) and the affective (emotions) inclinations of your child to have the mindset and the attitude assets, in knowing and living their lives as the *Bride of Christ*

At the end of this exploration, you will be able to:

- Provide and explain the scriptural indications of the Bride of Christ
- Indicate and clarify the biblical patterns using Adam and Eve, his wife, Isaac and Rebecca, his wife that show the Church, therefore your child as the Bride of Christ

- Describe and clarify the child's knowing and living in their identity as the Bride of Christ as an objective destination of Christian Formation
- Demonstrate your understanding of the implications of these lessons for your influence as parents in the early childhood Christian formation of your child

The Scriptural Indications of the Bride of Christ

- The Scripture does not provide a direct statement on the identity of the Church as the bride of Christ as it does with the Church as the body of Christ (Ephesians 4:15-16) - *But speaking the truth in love, may grow up into him in all things, which is the head, even Christ: From whom the whole body fitly joined together and compacted by that which every joint supplies, according to the effectual working in the measure of every part, makes increase of the body unto the edifying of itself in love.*
- However, by the Apostle Paul's teaching on Christian marriage in Ephesians 5:24-32, the Scripture shows that the Church as the body of Christ, and the Church as the wife/bride of Christ are two sides of the same coin, pertaining to her oneness with Christ. You cannot be the body of Christ and not be the wife/bride of Christ

<u>Please do a reading of Ephesians 5:24-32</u>

Husbands, love your wives, even as Christ also loved the church, and gave himself for it; that he might sanctify and cleanse it with the washing of water by the word, that he might present it to himself a glorious church, not having spot, or wrinkle, or any such thing; but that it should be holy and without blemish. So, ought men to love their wives as their own bodies. He that loves his wife loves himself. For no man ever yet hated his own flesh; but nourishes and cherishes it, even as the Lord the church: For we are members of his body, of his flesh, and of his bones. For this cause shall a man leave his father and mother, and shall be joined unto his wife, and they two shall be one flesh. This is a great mystery: but I speak concerning Christ and the Church.

- Paul's line of teaching in this scripture pinpoints Christ's dual oneness with the Church; (1) as a marital union, that is typical of a man and his wife, and (2) as in the couple joined in one flesh
- Below is an illustration of Christ's dual oneness with the Church

Figure 11. A representation of Christ dual oneness with the Church.

- Paul's teaching in Ephesians 5:24-32 presents the characteristics of Christ's marital union with the Church, as an example to be followed in the marital union of the man and his wife
- Paul's teaching brings out both the matrimonial and the anatomy/bodily structural view of Christ's oneness with the Church
- Indeed, it is in this teaching of Paul that brings out the Church's identity in her oneness with Christ as the wife/bride of Christ
- It affirms the significance in parenting the child from early childhood, which begins from the womb, to know and to live in their identity as the bride of Christ, as an essential destination in their Christian formation

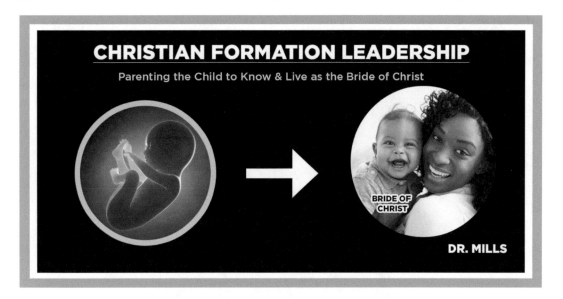

Figure 12. An illustration of viewing and valuing the parenting of your child to be the bride of Christ, starting from the womb.

The Biblical Patterns that Show the Church as the Bride of Christ

- In addition to these scriptural indications of the Church's identity as the bride of Christ, the Scripture also presents a biblical pattern in Adam and his wife Eve, in Isaac and his wife Rebecca; to show that the Church's identity as the bride of Christ is an objective God had eternally purposed for her oneness with Christ

Adam and Eve, his Wife

- There are scriptural references such as Romans 5:14, and the indications that Christ is the image of God (2 Corinthians 4:4, Colossians 1:15, and Hebrews 1:3) that suggest that the first Adam was made to represent both the physical and the spiritual personality of Christ as man

The Physical Personality of Christ as Man

Figure 13. A representation of the physical personality of Christ as man.

- It refers to the Physical human state of Christ; that is the person of Christ we are accustomed to in the New Testament scriptures, who was born to Joseph and Mary

The Spiritual Personality of Christ as Man

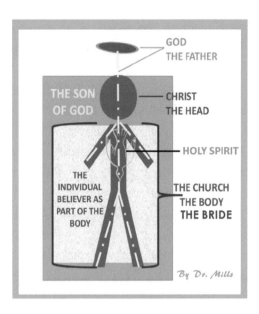

Figure 14. A representation of the spiritual personhood of
Christ as man (his oneness with the Church).

- It refers to the formed spiritual oneness of Christ and the Church, of which he is the 'head' of his body (Church) and at the same time the 'groom' of his wife/bride (Church). These two spiritual components of the oneness of Christ and the Church are inseparable, and in that union, it spiritually makes of Christ, one new person that the bible refers to as the one new man: Ephesians 2:14 -16 - *"For he is our peace, who hath made both one, and hath broken down the middle wall of partition between us; Having abolished in his flesh the enmity, even the law of commandments contained in ordinances; **for to make in himself of twain one new man**, so making peace; And that he might reconcile both unto God in one body by the cross, having slain the enmity thereby"*

We will now discuss how Adam and his wife Eve bring out the understanding of the Church/your child as the 'bride of Christ', which is the identity God has given to the Church/your child in the humanity of Christ.

Let us consider 2 Corinthians 4:4

In whom the god of this world hath blinded the minds of them which believe not, lest the light of **the glorious gospel of Christ, who is the image of God,** *should shine unto them.*

- You do realize in this verse, that the scripture treats Christ as the image of God. In other words, the image of God is Christ. This is to be an all-time truth about Christ's personhood as man
- The Greek word translated as image in the scripture is *eikon*. It means *'representation'*
- You also do realize in the scripture that the image of God is a reference specifically made to a person, who is Jesus Christ, and not to an inherent quality of God
- It then follows that eternally; Jesus Christ is and will always be the main point person for the full representation of the invincible God in his personality as man (Hebrews 1:3)
- You will soon come to learn that while Christ in his physical human state was indeed the image of God, spiritually, he is only a part of his inclusive representation of God with the Church, which would include your child
- Spiritually, Christ's representation of God included his oneness with the Church as his body and as his wife/bride, that was to come about after his death and resurrection

Let us now consider Genesis 1:26

And God said, let us make man in our image, after our likeness.

- The Hebrew word for 'image' used in Genesis 1:26 is *'tselem,'* which means a shadow/ representative figure/a copy of/a simulation
- You do realize in the way the scripture is put that God has an 'image' that we now know is Jesus Christ; both in his physical and spiritual personality as man
- We know this is so, because it is the personality of Christ as man that the Bible reveals is the express image of the invisible God (Hebrews 1:3). Christ also says about himself; *"If you have seen me, you have seen the Father,"* (John 14:6-9)
- It then follows that God is indicating in Genesis 1:26 that he is making man to be a resemblance of his image, whom we now know is Jesus Christ who was yet to come into the world as man

- The Apostle Paul supports this understanding of Adam being a resemblance of Christ with his statement in Romans 5:14 - "*Nevertheless, death reigned from Adam to Moses, even over them that had not sinned after the similitude **of Adam's transgression, who is the <u>figure of him that was to come</u>**.*"
- The Greek word for figure used in this verse is '*tupos*,' which literally means a shadow/a copy of/a simulation. It has the same meaning of the Hebrew word '*tselem*'
- You will soon learn that the Apostle Paul also treats Adam inclusively (the male and the female in oneness as man), as a shadow/representation of Christ's oneness with the Church

What are we establishing with this discussion?

- The first Adam (a oneness of two personalities as male and female) was created to be a shadow/a representation of Jesus Christ in accommodation of his oneness with the Church as his body and as his wife/bride

<u>Let us now consider Genesis 1:27</u>

So, God created man in his own image, in the image of God created he him; male and female created he them

- You realize in the scripture that the image of God is inclusively mentioned as male and female
- In Genesis 1:27, in making mankind to be a resemblance of Christ in his personality as man, God made the man male and female, as in Genesis 2:23-24 [*And the rib, which the LORD God had taken from man, made he a woman, and brought her unto the man. And Adam said, this is now bone of my bones, and flesh of my flesh: she shall be called Woman, because she was taken out of Man. Therefore, shall a man leave his father and his mother, and shall cleave unto his wife: and they shall be one flesh*]
- God did not make the man to co-exist just as male and female in their individual personalities, but he made them to be spiritually joined as one flesh, just as Christ and the Church is to be one flesh (Ephesians 5:30)

A Critical Question

Why did God Create Adam/Man male and Female?

Please do a reading of Ephesians 5:24-32

Husbands, love your wives, even as Christ also loved the church, and gave himself for it; that he might sanctify and cleanse it with the washing of water by the word, that he might present it to himself a glorious church, not having spot, or wrinkle, or any such thing; but that it should be holy and without blemish. So, ought men to love their wives as their own bodies. He that loves his wife loves himself. For no man ever yet hated his own flesh; but nourishes and cherishes it, even as the Lord the church: For we are members of his body, of his flesh, and of his bones. For this cause shall a man leave his father and mother, and shall be joined unto his wife, and they two shall be one flesh. This is a great mystery: but I speak concerning Christ and the Church.

- In Ephesians 5:24-32, it seems the Apostle Paul is making the claim that God's creation of mankind to be of a marital union as one flesh was based on what would be the marital nature of Christ's oneness with the Church as both his body and his bride
- Most probably, it was God's envisioned marital nature of Christ's oneness with the Church as both his body and wife that he created mankind male and female to be in marital union as one flesh, as Romans 5:14 seems to suggest
- At the same time, it was to serve as a copy/simulation/representation of the marital nature of Christ's oneness with the Church

The biblical analogy from Paul's Ephesians 5:24-32 is this:

What in Genesis 2, Eve was made to be for Adam as his own body and wife/bride is what God had eternally set the Church to be for Christ as his own body and wife/bride, affirming the Church's and therefore your child's identity in Christ as his bride.

Isaac and Rebecca his Wife

- There are several scriptural indications that suggest that as with Adam, Isaac was also a type of Christ pertaining to his Sonship to God, which also includes his oneness with the Church as his bride

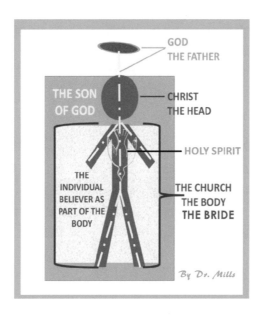

Figure 14. A representation of the spiritual personhood of
Christ as man (his oneness with the Church).

Please do a reading of the following scriptures

Genesis 24:61-67

And Rebecca arose, and her damsels, and they rode upon the camels, and followed the man: and the servant took Rebecca and went his way. And Isaac came from the way of the well Lahairoi; for he dwelt in the south country. And Isaac went out to meditate in the field at the eventide: and he lifted up his eyes, and saw, and, behold, the camels were coming. And Rebecca lifted up her eyes, and when she saw Isaac, she lighted off the camel. For she had said unto the servant, what man is this that walks in the field to meet us? And the servant had said, it is my master:

therefore, she took a vail, and covered herself. And the servant told Isaac all things that he had done. And Isaac brought her into his mother Sarah's tent, and took Rebecca, and she became his wife; and he loved her: and Isaac was comforted after his mother's death.

Hebrews 11:17-18

By faith Abraham, when he was tried, offered up Isaac: and he that had received the promises offered up his only begotten son, of whom it was said, That in Isaac shall thy seed be called: accounting that God was able to raise him up, even from the dead; from whence also he received him in a figure.

Romans 9:6-8

Not as though the word of God hath taken no effect. For they are not all Israel, which are of Israel: Neither, because they are the seed of Abraham, are they all children: but, In Isaac shall thy seed be called. That is, they which are the children of the flesh, these are not the children of God: but the children of the promise are counted for the seed.

Galatians 3:16

Now to Abraham and his seed were the promises made. He saith not, and to seeds, as of many; but as of one, and to thy seed, which is Christ.

Galatians 4:28

Now we, brethren, as Isaac was, are the children of promise.

Please do a reading of the following Watchman Nee's[2] commentary on Isaac as a figure of Christ

ISAAC AS A FIGURE OF CHRIST

But if Abraham was the father, immediately, we see Isaac as a figure of Christ the Son. No history so typifies Christ as does that of Isaac. Constituted the heir by divine promise, he was born, not after the flesh but after the spirit (Galatians 4: 29). Apart from Christ there was no other of whom this was said. Let us briefly recount some other ways in which Isaac may be a type of Christ. To Sarah, Isaac was Abraham's only true son, the beloved (Hebrews 11. 17). Laid by his father on the altar, he was received back as from the dead to be to him the risen one. After Sarah herself died and her 'age of grace' was past, Isaac's bride, a figure of the Church, was brought to him from a far country. Yet she came to him as the Church of God's will, not brought in from without but born from within, for Rebekah and Isaac were of one blood, one family, as are Christ and His own. Moreover, Isaac really did occupy his inheritance. Abraham at one point went down into Egypt and Jacob returned to Mesopotamia, but Isaac was born, lived, and died in Canaan. This is the Son who `is in heaven', who never left His Father's bosom. So, in remarkable detail Isaac is a type of Christ.

- In Watchman Nee's compelling commentary, as Isaac is a type of Christ, Rebecca is also a type of the Church
- As God presented Eve to the male Adam, (who is also a type of the son of God [Luke 3:38]), as his bride, God also presented Rebecca to Isaac to be his bride, as he is also presenting the Church to Christ to be his bride -*Husbands, love your wives, even as Christ also loved the church, and gave himself for it; that he might sanctify and cleanse it with the washing of water by the word, that he might present it to himself a glorious church, not having spot, or wrinkle, or any such thing; but that it should be holy and without blemish.* (Ephesians 5:25-27)

---

[2] Nee, W. (2007). Changed into his Likeness: CLC Publications.

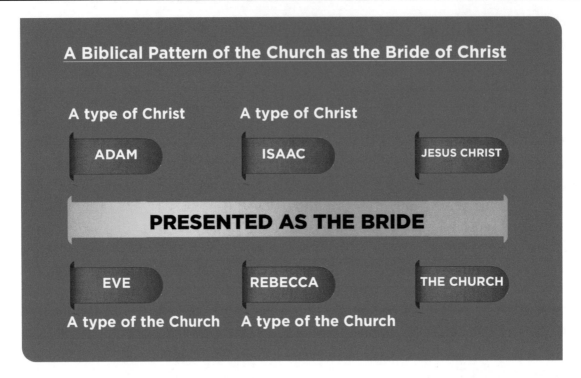

Figure 15. A biblical pattern of the Church as the bride of Christ.

- As with Adam and his wife, Eve, and as with Isaac and his wife, Rebecca, who are both a type of Christ and a type of the Church respectively, the Scripture develops the pattern to show that it was the intent and the everlasting purpose of God for the Church to be the bride of Christ

The Knowing and the Living as the Bride of Christ

- Given the biblical view that the Church is being formed in oneness with Christ as his bride, it should inform the task of Christian parenting to make the knowing and the living as the bride of Christ be an essential destination of the child's early childhood Christian formation, from conception through the first five formative years of the child

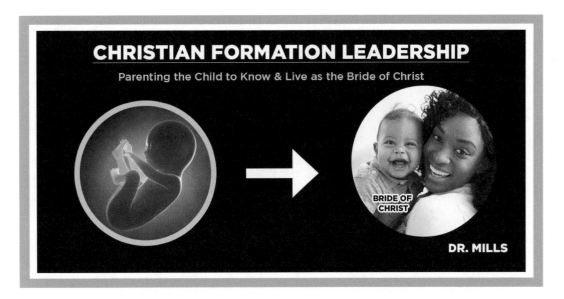

Figure 12. An illustration of viewing and valuing the parenting of your child to be the bride of Christ, starting from the womb.

- This understanding should prompt parents to give full diligence to the following considerations

Implication for Parents' Leadership in Christian Formation

- With guide from Romans 8:28-29, parenting the child to know and to live as the bride of Christ puts Christian parenting in alignment with the destination that God had preset/ordained for the Church's oneness with Christ as his bride
- An overarching objective of Christian parenting, therefore, is developing the cognitive and the affective inclinations of the child to gain the mindset and emotional assets (the attitude sets), to know and to live in their identity as the bride of Christ, as did the parents of Sampson (to know and to live as a Nazarite)
- Parents' openness to the Christian formation techniques for the early childhood Christian formation of the child, from conception through the first five formative years, to know and to live as the bride of Christ is a duty/ministry of grace to their own child's Christian formation

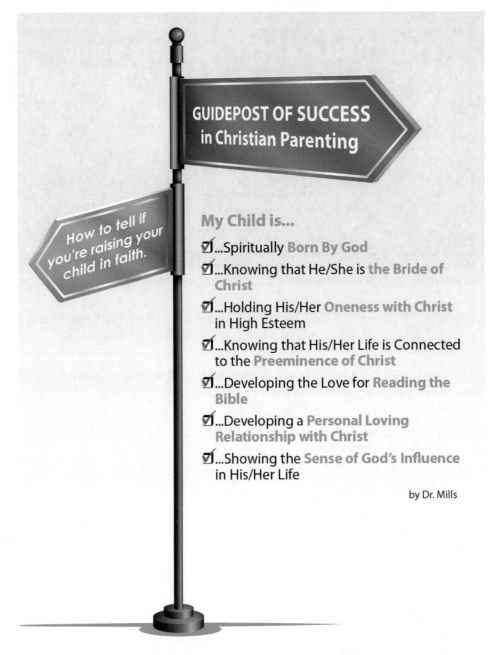

Figure 16. Dr. Mills guidepost of success in Christian parenting.

- Dr. Mills' Guidepost of Success in Christian Parenting provides some checkpoints that show the signs that your parenting is helping your child realize the benchmarks God had laid out in his eternal purpose for bringing them into the world
- You do realize that the Guidepost of Success in Christian Parenting includes the children knowing that they are the Bride of Christ, and showing the consciousness of God's influence in their lives
- Remember the child is not yours. They belong to God. You are to parent the child into becoming what God had desired for them to be, in their oneness with Christ

A thing to Consider

The 3rd-Point Principle of Christian Parenting points to the order that the parenting goals and objectives for the children are to be pinned on what God had purposed their lives to be in their oneness with Christ, as his body and bride.

True or False

Discussion

Please discuss with your spouse, the parenting of your child in their God given identity as the bride of Christ, if it applies.

PERSONAL GROWTH ASSESSMENT

Please write in the space provided the lessons that you have gained from this chapter of your study

_____

_____

_____

_____

_____

_____

_____

_____

_____

_____

_____

CHAPTER 4

FORMATION

Developing the Identity and the Lifestyle of the Child as Set by God

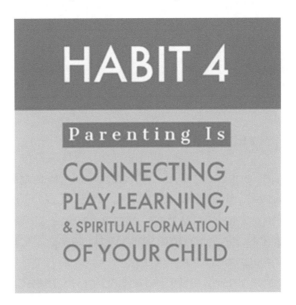

Please do a Reading of the Following Recap

You now know that parents are God's portal for the entrance of the child he has earmarked for the formation of Christ's oneness with the Church. The logic that follows is also clear that parents are, therefore, God's stewards of the child. The child is God's property and not yours. You also have in your understanding that your parenting is to be pinned on what God has designated the identity and the lifestyle of the child to be, in their oneness with Christ. God's designated identity of the child in their oneness with Christ is given as the body and the bride of Christ. God's designated lifestyle for the child is the Christ's life with the Father's influence that he modeled. The 4th-point principle is being about the formation or the development of the child's identity and the lifestyle designated by God in their oneness with Christ.

A Guiding Question

What lessons can be gleaned from Sampson's parents that project the significance of this principle in Christian parenting?

The Example with Sampson's Parents

Please do a Reading of Judges 13:12

And Manoah said to the angel, "Now let thy words come to pass. How shall we order the child, and how shall we do unto him?"

The Lessons from Sampson's Parents

- Manoah's request brings out their sense of what their parenting influence in the child was to entail, besides providing his basic needs, such as food, clothing, and wellness
- Manoah's request seemed to show that their awareness was greatly present that there were a set of activities they were to do to and with Sampson, in forming his life to become the person God had designated him to be
- Manoah's request also seemed to show he had in his mental attitude, the principle that for Sampson to turn out to become what God had designated his life to be, it will require a habit formation by doing a set of activities with him

Sampson's Habit Formation as a Nazarite to God

- We will examine Sampson's habit formation as a Nazarite to God through the lens of educational psychology
- Today, the School of Psychology and Learning has given us the knowledge currency that there are three principal learning domains in human development that form our behavioral functions
- These learning domains are the cognitive (mindsets), affective (emotions/attitude assets), and psychomotor (motor skills) functions of the child

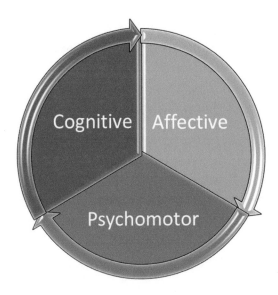

Figure 17. The three learning domains in educational psychology.

- Tons of studies, research, and information in psychology is present to show that soundness in human behavior relates to the set of activities that are diligently done in the developmental milestones of each of these learning domains in the child's human development
- These are systems of learning that I believe will tremendously be helpful to you as Christian parents and your parenting influence in the early childhood Christian formation of your child, from the womb through the formative years of the child

Please do a Reading of Judges 16:17

And it came to pass, when she pressed him daily with her words, and urged him, so that his soul was vexed unto death; that he told her all his heart, and said unto her, there has not come a razor upon mine head; for I have been a Nazarite unto God from my mother's womb.

- In Sampson's words, we can attribute his habit as a Nazarite to what seemed to be the formation of his cognitive, affective, and psychomotor behavioral assets to know and to live as a Nazarite unto God. **What are these assets**?

COGNITIVE: The formed knowledge/the knowing and the reckoning of his identity that he is a Nazarite unto God

AFFECTIVE: The formed emotional attitude or his disposition to live the set lifestyle as a Nazarite to God

PSYCHOMOTOR: To not have had razor touched his hair from early childhood into his adulthood

- Manoah and his wife may not have had the knowledge currency of these learning domains as behavioral assets that relate to sound human development as we do today
- For Sampson to live as a Nazarite unto God from early childhood through his adulthood was certainly not a random habit formation
- It was fully the result of the diligent influence of his parents, more likely, using parenting techniques that will shape his mindsets, and emotional assets (attitude sets) to live that Nazarite lifestyle, as an influence of God in his life

The Lessons for Christian Parents

- The knowledge in psychology concerning the three learning domains (cognitive, affective, and psychomotor) in human development is to be rewarding for you and your parenting influence in the early childhood Christian formation of your own children

Please think on the Scripture in Philippians 2:13

For it is God who works in you both to will and to do of his good pleasure.

Please Consider the Following Assessments of the Scripture

To will – human volition [the cognitive and the affective process by which an individual decides on and commits to a task]

To do – human motor control [The signals from the nervous system that causes an individual to make directed bodily movements to carry out a task].

- You do realize how by the Holy Spirit, God influences the human cognitive, affective, and psychomotor functions to get us to favorably respond to his desires and directives?
- The scriptural assessment of Philippians 2:13 can be linked with Proverbs 22:6 – *"Train up a child in the way he should go: and when he is old, he will not depart from it."*
- The Hebrew word for *train* used in this scripture is '***Chanak***.' The Strong's Lexicon translates it to connote, *to dedicate*, which implies the disciplining of the child to live in a certain way
- The Macmillandictionary.com offers this definition for the word *train – to make mind and body do something*
- The two scriptural points do merge to give the prospects for developing the cognitive, affective, and the motor sets of the child, from early childhood to meet the ideals of Christian formation, through parenting

What is the idealism of Christian formation?

In Dr. Mills' words, *"the art and science in forming the mindset and the emotional asset (the attitude set) of a child, to become a member of the body of Christ, hence, the bride of Christ; so that in adulthood, the individual has a formed lifestyle of strong consciousness for the personal presence and influence of God in the management of their Christian lives."*.

- The School of Psychology, and the example of Sampson's parents do serve the point that as Christian parents, you can engage your children in targeted learning activities as early in the womb to develop their cognitive, affective, and psychomotor sets to proudly know and live as the bride of Christ and to have strong influence of God in their day-to-day Christian living

The Crawling - Walking Child

Connecting play, learning and spiritual formation

DR. MILLS

This parenting technique, The Crawling-Walking Child, for example provides parents with the techniques they can use to develop the coordination of the child's cognition, affective, and motor sets during the crawling and early walking stages of their developmental milestones, to form their habit in trusting, loving. and reading the Bible. It is also to develop the attitude and motor sets of the child, for a growing and loving personal relationship with Jesus Christ.

Key Lessons - The Take-Away

- Effectual Parenting requires things that parents are to do to, and with the child to develop the appropriate habits due for their Christian living from the womb, early childhood, through adulthood
- Parenting techniques are the set of activities parents are to do to, and with the child for the child's early childhood cognitive, affective, and psychomotor development, for the realization of the set goals and objectives, for their Christian formation

A thing to Consider

Manoah's request from God concerning the parenting of Sampson shows he had in his mental attitude the principle that for Sampson to turn out to become what God had designated his life to be, it will require a habit formation by doing a set of activities with him.

True or False

Discussion

Please discuss with your spouse, the routine things you are to do to and with your child's early childhood Christian formation as the bride of Christ and to have the personal influence of God in their lives, if it applies.

PERSONAL GROWTH ASSESSMENT

Please write in the space provided the lessons that you have gained from this chapter of your study

_____

_____

_____

_____

_____

_____

_____

_____

_____

_____

_____

_____

CHAPTER 5

TEAMWORK

A Joint Effort of Both Parents (Where it Applies)

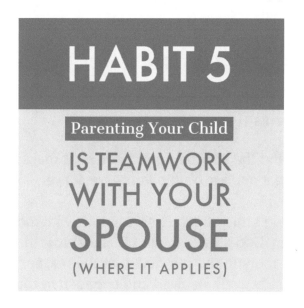

<u>A Guiding Question</u>

What lessons can be gleaned from Sampson's parents that project the significance of this principle in Christian parenting?

The Example with Sampson's Parents

Please do a Reading of Judges 13:8

Then Manoah intreated the LORD, and said, O my Lord, let the man of God which thou didst send come again unto us and teach us what we shall do unto the child that shall be born.

The Lessons from Sampson's Parents

- You do realize from the scripture that the two parents were both actively involved or together as a team for the parenting of Sampson
- They came into one mind or mental attitude in parenting Sampson to be and to live as a Nazarite
- Manoah's leadership as the husband and the father in bringing the family together to entreat God for his desired parenting of Sampson was outstanding and worthy of emulation

The Lesson for Christian Parents

- The art and science and the spiritual aspects of what makes for Christian parenting are effectual, when where it applies, both parents are actively involved and engaged in it as a team
- God gives grace for single parenting. However, as it is with most things affected in creation
- by the depravity of sin, God always shows his archetypes/his desired original standards
- By God's design, it is more in the principle that the nucleus family functions at its best, when both parents are actively involved and engaged in the parenting of the child, as a team
- Manoah's leadership as a husband and a father for the parenting of Sampson is to inspire and motivate fathers in Christian homes to give the leadership that unites the family through prayer and the openness to God to search, to study and to receive the training needed for the effectual parenting of the child

The Benefit in Parenting the Child as a Team

When in principle, parents take on a joint effort to diligently parent their children as a team, according to the eternal purpose that God had purposed concerning Christ's oneness with the Church, it is rewarding in the following effects:

- It helps you as parents **to have the same mind** in parenting the child to know and to live as the bride of Christ, and for them to have the developed consciousness for the influence of God in the management of their Christian living
- As parents, working as a team in the parenting of your child will most likely bolster your oneness as husband and wife
- It will most likely, achieve a positive spiral impact on the strengths of your immediate society and possibly, further – a studier nucleus family, safer neighborhoods, stronger communities, safe city, strong state, and a Godly Nation

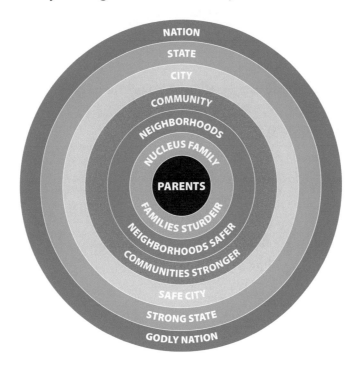

Figure 18. The spiral effect of Christian parenting.

- The spiral effect of effectual Christian parenting is to give you the portrait to visualize the extent of your influence, when you give the due diligence to the 6-Point Principles of Christian Parenting, as the habits of highly effective parents
- You do realize that your position as parents and your parenting influence in the early childhood Christian formation of your child is an invaluable pathway for advancing the Church's witness of Christ, and effecting positive social change in your neighborhood, city, state, and nation
- **Please Remember**: This spiral effect rests significantly on parenting the child as a team that would fortify your oneness as husband and wife and the strengthening of your nucleus family

A thing to Consider

A fortified oneness of husband and wife in the parenting of their child as a team usually corresponds to a positive spiral impact on the strengths of their immediate society.

True or False

In principle, it is expedient for the father in a Christian home to give the leadership that unites the family through prayer and the openness to God to search, to study and to receive the training needed for the effectual parenting of the child.

True or False

Discussion

Please discuss with your spouse, the values, and the effort you are to put in, in the parenting of your child as a teamwork, if it applies.

PERSONAL GROWTH ASSESSMENT

Please write in the space provided the lessons that you have gained from this chapter of your study

_____

_____

_____

_____

_____

_____

_____

_____

_____

_____

_____

_____

CHAPTER 6

TRAINING

Parenting Skills Development

A Guiding Question

What lessons can be gleaned from Sampson's parents that project the significance of this principle in Christian parenting?

The Example with Sampson's Parents

Please do a Reading of Judges 13:8

Then Manoah intreated the LORD, and said, O my Lord, let the man of God which thou didst send come again unto us, and **teach us** *what we shall do unto the child that shall be born.*

The Lessons from Sampson's Parents

- You do realize the parents were not simply after information on parenting. They were in pursuit of God to learn from him, the tools/techniques they are to use that will do the job of parenting Sampson to become of the identity and the lifestyle that God had set for him to be and to have
- The Hebrew word '**teach**' used in this scripture is 'yara,' and connotes instructing someone how to do something
- The parents had an attitude of receptiveness to learning, for the sake of achieving effectiveness and efficiency in their parenting of Sampson

The Lessons for Christian Parents

- By now, it should have become firm in you that as parents, you are God's primary ministers not only for the child's entrance into the world, but also for them to come into their identity in Christ [the bride of Christ] and to have the lifestyle of Christ [the influence of God in their Christian living]
- As the primary ministers of God for the child's formation in Christ, it should be apparent in you that Christian parenting requires effectual work - a set of activities that you are to do to and with the child, as early from conception

The Crawling/Walking Child - Parenting Techniques.

- Effectual work of Christian parenting means using the techniques needed for the development of the child's cognitive, affective, and psychomotor assets at the various stages of their human development to come into their identity and the lifestyle God had set for them in being formed to have oneness with Christ
- Sampson's parents set the example for our receptiveness to training and skill development for the effectual parenting of the child's Christian formation
- As the primary ministers of God for the child's formation in Christ, the scripture admonishes us in 2 Timothy 2:15: *"Study to shew thyself approved unto God, a workman that needs not to be ashamed...*
- As the primary ministers of God 2 Timothy 2:15 is the scriptural invitation for you to seek and to receive parenting skills development, for the effectual early childhood Christian formation of the child's God approved identity and lifestyle in Christ

PERSONAL GROWTH ASSESSMENT

Please write in the space provided the lessons that you have gained from this chapter of your study

_____

_____

_____

_____

_____

_____

_____

_____

_____

_____

_____

_____

In not Leaving your Child to Chance!

Do you know why God, the Father is bringing or has brought 'your' child into the world, by you as their parents? Are you sure on the fact that God, the Father is the main stakeholder on what your child is to become and the lifestyle they are to have and to live on earth? As parents, what good does it serve to find out that your fulfilled personal aspirations in your child are not in line with the stakes God, the Father had preset for them? You will find in the Bible that it is not always a pleasant discovery. An example is Abraham's birthing and upbringing of Ishmael. I believe you will not want that to happen to you!!

Albeit, do you know how much God values you as parents, for the life of your child? There is a principle in this book that I will like you to ponder over for a moment - *As God has ordered things to be in creation for certain specific functions, he has also rendered it certain in creation that without parents, his mission to form Christ's oneness with the Church cannot happen; since parents are God's created portals for bringing into the world the child who will become one with Christ, as a member of the Church; therefore, his body and bride.*

And so, what you have in your hand is this:

The book – 'The Six Habits of Highly Effective Parents,' which comprise a 6-Point Principles of Christian Parenting. In it, you will learn the powerful lessons that will help you **succeed** in aligning your parenting with the eternal mission, objective, and the eternal vision of God, for entrusting your child into your hands, Selah!

The Author

Samuel Kirk Mills, EDD
President & CEO – *Global Institute for Christian Living and Growth.*

Samuel Kirk Mills, EDD is an alumnus of Moody Bible Institute, Wheaton Graduate School (Billy Graham Scholar), and Northern Illinois University. In his 40 plus years of Christian Ministry, Dr. Mills is endowed with extensive biblical insights and applications for successful Christian living and growth.

'The Six Habits of Highly Effective Parents' is a passion to have parents succeed in their influence for the early childhood Christian formation of their own children, for the global influence of the Church. He is married to Nana. They have two young adults – Naa Koshie and Nii Odartey.

ADDITIONAL RESOURCES

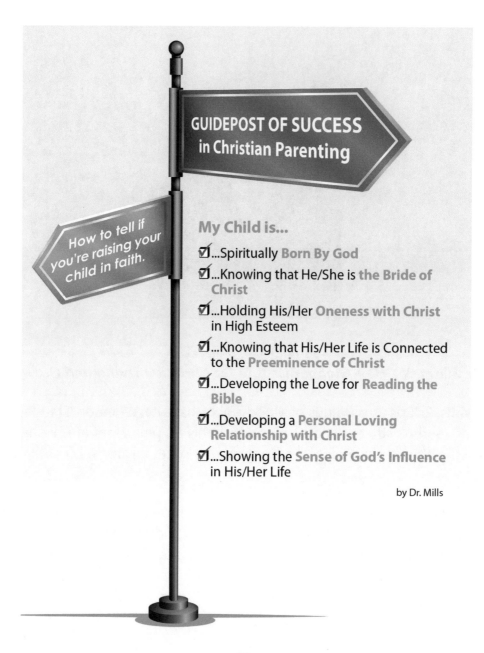

GUIDEPOST OF SUCCESS
in Christian Parenting

How to tell if you're raising your child in faith.

My Child is...

☑ ...Spiritually **Born By God**

☑ ...Knowing that He/She is **the Bride of Christ**

☑ ...Holding His/Her **Oneness with Christ** in High Esteem

☑ ...Knowing that His/Her Life is Connected to the **Preeminence of Christ**

☑ ...Developing the Love for **Reading the Bible**

☑ ...Developing a **Personal Loving Relationship with Christ**

☑ ...Showing the **Sense of God's Influence** in His/Her Life

by Dr. Mills

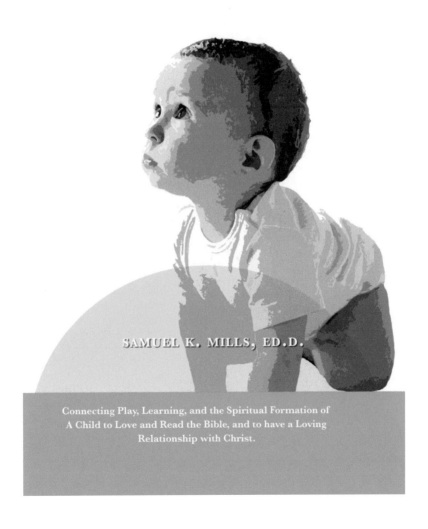

The Crawling / Walking Child

PARENTING TECHNIQUES HANDBOOK

SAMUEL K. MILLS, ED.D.

Connecting Play, Learning, and the Spiritual Formation of
A Child to Love and Read the Bible, and to have a Loving
Relationship with Christ.

The Bible, Our Friend

Written By Samuel Kirk Mills, ED.D.
Illustrations By Adrian Golden

Printed in the United States
by Baker & Taylor Publisher Services